I0648851

John Lubbock, Thomas Kerslake, J. Bryce

Mr. Gladstone and the Nationalities of the United Kingdom

John Lubbock, Thomas Kerslake, J. Bryce

Mr. Gladstone and the Nationalities of the United Kingdom

ISBN/EAN: 9783337132897

Printed in Europe, USA, Canada, Australia, Japan

Cover: Foto ©ninafisch / pixelio.de

More available books at **www.hansebooks.com**

MR. GLADSTONE

AND THE

NATIONALITIES OF THE UNITED KINGDOM.

A Series of Letters to the " Times "

BY

SIR JOHN LUBBOCK, BART., M.P., F.R.S., D.C.L., LL.D.

President of the Linnean Society, First President of the Anthropological Institute, Trustee of the British Museum.

WITH REJOINDERS BY MR. J. BRYCE, M.P.,

AND LETTERS IN SUPPORT BY

THE DUKE OF ARGYLL, DR. JOHN BEDDOE, &c.

FOLLOWED BY

"Gyfla : the Scir of the Ivel Valley,"

BY THOMAS KERSLAKE;

AND THE CORRESPONDENCE WHICH IT HAS ELICITED.

****

LONDON :

BERNARD QUARITCH, 15 PICCADILLY.

1887.

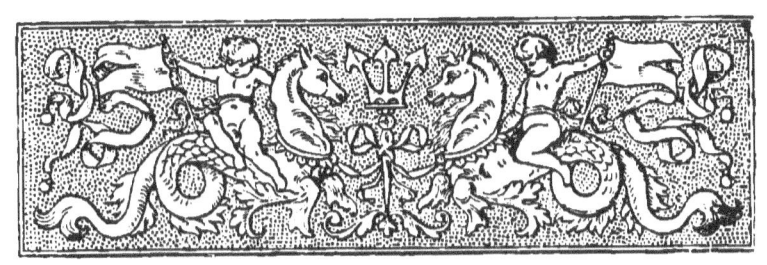

INTRODUCTION.

IN reprinting the interesting Letters of SIR JOHN LUBBOCK, Bart., M.P., to the *Times*, on the subject of the NATIONALITIES and RACES of GREAT BRITAIN and IRELAND, and the replies they elicited from MR. BRYCE, M.P., the DUKE OF ARGYLL, and others, I believe that I am doing a service to politicians and historical students.

As an Appendix to that Correspondence, I reprint a pamphlet (" Gyfla," 9 pp., 1887) of my friend THOMAS KERSLAKE, the spirited antiquary, formerly one of my most intelligent rivals in the old-book trade, with the correspondence to which it has led.

I take the opportunity here of making a remark which has a close bearing upon the subject-matter of the following pages. It is a singular fact, that whilst in distant rural and mountainous districts, both in this country and on the Continent, we find whole villages bearing the same typical physiognomy, we meet in London and other large English towns with types of all the races which have settled in this country. Even in a single family, children of the same parents are frequently so different as to betoken clearly the original elements of their mixed Teutonic and Celtic descent; while in the lower classes of the London populace not only the Celtic, but even its forerunner, the Iberian, type seems to be largely reproduced.

MR. GLADSTONE AND THE NATIONALITIES OF THE UNITED KINGDOM.

To the Editor of the " Times."

Sir,—I observe that the supporters of Home Rule place in the forefront of their argument the assertion that "we have within the compass of the United Kingdom no less than four real nationalities." By this I do not suppose that allusion is meant to the modern and, so to say, accidental divisions between England and Scotland in the first place, England and Wales in the second, or to the silver streak between Britain and Ireland, for we are hardly so degenerate as to reverse our old boast and allow the waves to rule Britannia. In fact, the addition of the adjective "real" is, of course, intended to give emphasis to the declaration, which no doubt means that there are in the United Kingdom four distinct races, and that the existence of four distinct races is reason why we should permit one of them to have a separate Legislature and a separate Executive. It is, therefore, worth while to inquire what the facts really are. As regards South Britain, it will be generally admitted that, omitting the question of pre-Celtic races (though these form, I believe, a far more important element in our population than is generally recognised), Wales and Cornwall are predominantly Celtic ; that the south and east are predominantly Anglo-Saxon, with a considerable Norman intermixture ; that certain districts are mainly Scandinavian ; that our population is built up of three principal elements—Celtic, Anglo-Saxon, and Scandinavian.

In Ireland the population of the east and north is mainly Saxon, in the north-west Celtic, while in the extreme south-west the basis is Iberian, akin to the population of parts of Spain. Very many of those who imagine themselves to be Celts, and the natural foes of the Sassenach, are descendants of English colonists, even in Munster and Connaught. The Parnells, Grays, Moores, Burkes, Fitzgeralds, Barrys, Butlers, and, according to some, the McMahons, are Anglo-Norman.

I pass to North Britain. Here we are met at once by the curious fact that the Saxons entered Caledonia, if not before, at any rate about the same time as, the Scots. In fact the Scots were an Irish tribe. Ireland, says Bede, "was the original country of the Scots"—"Ibernia propria Scotorum est patria." "Scotia was originally Ireland," said Bozius,—"Scotia, quæ tum erat Ibernia." The Scot came from Ireland, says Marianus,—"Scotus, de Ibernia insula natus." Ireland, says Chalmers in his great work, was "known at the end of the third century as the native country of the Scots, and in after-ages by the name of Scotland; this appellation was afterwards transferred from Ireland to Scotland"; and he asserts, as the result of all his inquiries, that no permanent settlement of the Scots in Caledonia took place till towards the close of the sixth century.

In fact, down to the Middle Ages, if a person was called a Scot, it was meant that he was born in Ireland. I must not overwhelm you with quotations, but having given several of the earliest authorities, perhaps you will allow me to quote two of the latest. Mr. Bonwick says, "the real Scotia was Ireland, whose name got transferred to North Britain," and Mr. Taylor, in "Words and Places," remarks that "the Scots, this

c

conquering Irish sept, which appears to have actually colonised only a part of Argyle, succeeded in bestowing its name on the whole country." Argyle is indeed the country of the Gael or Irishman. In the North of Scotland, the Orkneys, and Shetlands, the population is mainly Scandinavian, Sutherland being so named as the southern portion of their territory. In the east and south the population is mainly Anglo-Saxon. Edinburgh is an Anglo-Saxon city, built by Edwin, King of Northumbria, and called after him.

Of the great Scotch families, the Baliols came from Bailleul or Baliol in Normandy, the Bruces from Yorkshire, the Stewarts from Shropshire, the Hamiltons from Hambleton in Buckinghamshire, the Lindsays from Lindsay in Essex, the Sinclairs from St. Clair in Normandy, the Comyns from Comines in Flanders. Some even of the Highland clans are Teutonic. According to some authorities, the Camerons derive their name from Cambronne. The Gordons, says MacLaughlan, the Frasers, the Chisholms, &c., are without any trace of a connection with the Celts, and originally without doubt of purely Teutonic blood; while the Maclaughlans, Kennedys, Macdonalds, and Munroes are Irish, and the Elliotts, Frasers, Maxwells, Mathesons, and Keiths English.

"The great heroes of Scottish history," says Bonwick, " Bruce and Wallace, were of English origin." The Lothians, says Hume, were "entirely peopled with Saxons."

Thus, then, in Scotland, as in England, the east is mainly Teutonic, the west mainly Celtic.

Huxley and Beddoe have both pointed out, and it will be generally admitted, that the people north and south of the line dividing England and Scotland are practically identical. On the other hand, so far from Scotland being inhabited by a single homogeneous people, the struggle between the east and west was bitter and prolonged. The Wolf of Badenoch and his Highlanders burned Elgin in 1390 ; and, says Burton, "it will be difficult to make those not familiar with the tone of feeling in Lowland Scotland at that time believe that the defeat of Donald of the Isles (at Harlaw) was felt as a more memorable deliverance even than that of Bannockburn."

I maintain, therefore, that the defence of Home Rule, on the ground that there are four "real nationalities" in our islands is entirely without foundation. If, however, we are to be divided at all according to blood, the divisions would not be into England, Scotland, Ireland, and Wales. The main division in Great Britain would be not from east to west, but from north to south ; the Saxon division would include the greater portion of the east of England, the east of Ireland, and of Scotland ; the Celtic division would comprise most of the west of Ireland and west of Scotland, with Wales and Cornwall ; the Scandinavian the north of Scotland, several maritime districts on the east, Westmoreland, Cumberland, and Pembroke, while the extreme south-west of Ireland and part of Wales would be Iberian. The exact limits would give rise to an endless number of bitter disputes.   Indeed, so much intermingled are the different races that one of our highest authorities, Dr. Beddoe, after careful and prolonged study, says :— "With respect to the distribution and commixture of race elements in the British Isles, we may safely assert that not one of them, whether Iberian, Gaelic, Cymric, Saxon, or Scandinavian, is peculiar to, or absent from, or everywhere predominant in any one of the three kingdoms."

This being so, I submit that any argument in favour of Home Rule based on the existence of distinct nationalities falls utterly to the ground, while the effect of rousing race antagonisms, from which we have suffered so terribly in the past, and which are now happily latent, can only add to our political difficulties and tend to weaken the British Empire; while, on the contrary, if we recognise the undeniable ethnological fact that English, Irish, and Scotch are all composed of the same elements, and in not very dissimilar proportions, it would do much to mitigate our unfortunate dissensions, and add to the strength and welfare of our common country.

I am, Sir, your obedient servant,

JOHN LUBBOCK.

HOUSE OF COMMONS.

[*" Times," March* 18, 1887.]

To THE EDITOR OF THE "TIMES."

SIR,—In his interesting letter to you Sir John Lubbock entirely misses the bearing of Mr. Gladstone's remark by confusing races with nationalities. A nationality may be made up of any number of races, because race is only one of several elements which go to create a nationality. Everybody knows that from the fifth to the tenth century "Scotus" meant an Irishman. Everybody knows that the Scottish people consist of four or five races—Picts, Scots, Angles,

Northmen, Strathclyde Britons. But that does not make the Scotch any the less a nation, because history has slowly fused these various races into a cohesive whole. So the Swiss are both a nationality and a nation, although they spring from several races, and four languages are still spoken within their borders. The same may be said of the French and the Germans.

It would take too long to point out the minor statements of Sir J. Lubbock's letter, which seem to be either very doubtful or erroneous, so I will only observe, in passing, that the Saxons were not in Caledonia before the Scots; that the name Argyle has nothing to do with the Gael, nor the Camerons with Cambronne; that in Sutherland there is very little Scandinavian blood; that there is no reason to think the Kennedys, Munroes, and so forth, to be Irish; that although Bruce, the claimant of the Scottish throne, was an Anglo-Norman, the name Bruce is Norwegian (Brusi), and probably most of the Scottish Bruces are descendants of Norwegian settlers; and that William Wallace was not an Englishman, but, if we are to go by his name at all, a Welshman—*i.e.*, a Strathclyde Briton.

The point of Mr. Gladstone's remarks seems to me to be, that in a question involving national sentiment the opinion of each of the nationalities surviving in our islands is worth regarding ; and that the people of Scotland and Wales, still cherishing a distinct national feeling of their own, though one happily compatible with attachment to the greater nationality of the United Kingdom, have shown that they can extend their sympathy to the sentiment of nationality among the Irish, and that they do not deem it dangerous to Imperial unity. An Englishman has but one patriotism, because England and the United Kingdom are to him practically the same thing. A Scotchman has two, but he is sensible of no opposition between them. He is none the less loyal to the United Kingdom because he is also loyal to Scotland. And he believes the day may come when the same will be true of an Irishman.

I am, Sir, faithfully yours,

March 19.   J. BRYCE.

["*Times,*" *March* 21, 1887.]

To the Editor of the "Times."

Sir,—I am very glad that my letter has so far effected its object as to have extracted, from one of the most eminent advocates of Home Rule, the ad-

mission that the argument in support of separate
Legislatures for England, Scotland, Ireland, and
Wales, based on the supposed existence of four
" real nationalities," in the sense of there being four
distinct races occupying these four geographical
regions, is entirely without foundation. Of course,
I do not imagine that Professor Bryce ever supposed
that there were such distinct races, but thousands of
people not so well informed have so understood the
argument.

Professor Bryce, however, having entirely admitted
my contention, proceeds to enumerate some points
which he states to be either very doubtful or erroneous. He gives, indeed, no evidence in support of
his statements, still you will perhaps allow me to
defend myself.

The points on which he contradicts my statements
are (1) the origin of Sir W. Wallace ; (2) the origin
of the Bruces ; (3) that Argyle was called after the
Gaels ; (4) that the Saxons were in Scotland before,
or as soon as, the Scots ; (5) that Sutherland was so
named from its relation to the Scandinavian settlements in the Orkneys and Shetlands; (6) that the
name Cameron is derived from Cambronne; and (7)
that the Kennedys and Munroes are of Irish origin.

As regards the first point, Mr. Bryce asserts that Wallace "was not an Englishman, but, if we are to go by his name at all, a Welshman." But what says Chalmers? "The original country," he states, "of this great man's family is idly supposed to be Wales; but his progenitors were undoubtedly an Anglo-Norman family." . . "The Scottish antiquaries suppose," he adds, "the families of Wallace and Valoines, who both came from England into Scotland, to have been the same; but that these two families were distinct is apparent."

Speaking of Wallace, Sir Walter Scott, in his History, says, " This champion of his country was of Anglo-Norman descent."

Secondly, Mr. Bryce questions the assertion that Bruce was Anglo-Norman. " Robert de Brus or Bruce," says Burton, " was a cadet of Norman family, powerful among the baronial houses of the North of England."

" Robert de Bruis," says Chalmers, " was an opulent baron in Yorkshire at the epoch of the Domesday Book." I do not doubt that the family are originally Scandinavian, but this does not affect the question.

Thirdly, Mr. Bryce asserts that "the name Argyle

had nothing to do with the Gael." " The old Scotch form of Argyle," says Skene, "is Earrgaoidheal, from ' earr,' a limit or boundary, and this approaches most nearly to the form of the name in the old descriptions, with its etymology of margin or limit of the Gael."

"Argyle," says Chalmers, "signified merely the limit or boundary of the Irishmen or Gael."

" Here also," says Rhys ("Celtic Britain"), "may be mentioned Argyle, as it is found variously called Oirir Gaethel, Airer Gaethel, and Arregaethel, meaning the region belonging to the Goidel, or Gaelic-speaking people."

"The name Gael," says Taylor, in "Words and Places," was used "as a national appellation by the Gaels of Caledonia and the Gauls of Gallia. Galway, Donegal, Galloway, and Argyle are Gaelic districts."
"Northern Argyle," says Robertson, "was that portion of the territories of the Oirir-Gael which reached from the northern boundaries of the modern county to the frontiers of the Gall-Gael," and in his map the district is marked as Oirir-Gael.

Fourthly, Professor Bryce asserts that the Saxons were not in Scotland before the Celts. Chalmers says, " The Britons were the first, the Saxons were the

second people, whose descendants have finally pre-
vailed over the posterity of the other two ; and the
Irish-Scots were the third race." Professor Bryce
will, I think, admit at any rate that there was no
great difference in point of time.

Fifthly, I stated that Sutherland was so named by
the Scandinavians. On the contrary, says Mr. Bryce,
" in Sutherland there is very little Scandinavian
blood." In support of my assertion I may again
quote Isaac Taylor, who says—" It may seem strange
that the extreme north-western corner of Great
Britain should be called Sutherland. No inhabitant
of Scotland could have bestowed so inappropriate
a name. The name of Sutherland was evidently
given by a people living still further to the north.
Here, as well as in Caithness, we find numerous
Norwegian names." In the map he gives, the
straths and glens of Sutherland are coloured as
Norwegian.

The Scandinavians, says Burton, "spread over the
northern mainland, occupying large tracts in Caithness and Sutherland." Caithness and Sutherland,
says Skene, " became more Norwegian than Scotch,"
and again, " in 989 Sigurd was in possession of the
four provinces of Moray, Ross, Sudrland or Suther-

land, and Dali." The descendants of the Scandinavians, says Chalmers, " may still be distinguished within Caithness and Sutherland, as a distinct race of Gothic people, from the Saxon inhabitants of the more southern districts."

His other two points are of minor interest, but if space permitted I should have been prepared to support my statements by ample evidence. I think, however, that I have said enough to vindicate myself from the charge of inaccuracy, which my friend must forgive me for saying he has too hastily brought against me.

It is very satisfactory to find that Mr. Bryce does not attempt to maintain that any argument in favour of Home Rule can be based on difference of race. In truth, Celts, Anglo-Saxons, and Scandinavians people in no very different proportions, and with no fixed or clear boundaries, England and Scotland and Ireland alike.

One word in conclusion. Race, says Mr. Bryce, " is only one of several elements which go to create a nationality." History, he adds, " may slowly fuse " various races into a cohesive whole." Is this, then, now his argument? Has history done so in the case of Ireland? Does he really maintain that Ulster is fused into a cohesive whole with the rest of the island ? If not, then surely the second argument is as untenable as the first.

I am, Sir, your obedient servant,

JOHN LUBBOCK.

HOUSE OF COMMONS, *March* 21.

[" *Times" Supplement, March* 25, 1887.]

TO THE EDITOR OF THE " TIMES."

SIR,—In the concluding paragraph of the letter from Mr. J. Bryce, which appears in your columns of this day, he points to Scotland as a country cherishing a distinct national feeling of its own in conjunction with loyalty and attachment to a greater nationality, and he looks forward to the growth of a similar state of sentiment in Ireland. It may, therefore, be worth while to remind Mr. Bryce that his satisfaction with the present condition of national feeling in Scotland is not shared by his political confederate, Mr. Parnell, and that the ideal contemplated by the Irish Nationalist

leader would seem to be a very different one. " Scotland" (said Mr. Parnell on September 1, 1885, in
response to the toast of " Ireland a Nation " at a
banquet in the Dublin Mansion-house) " has lost her
nationality, and has practically become merged in
England ; but Ireland has never done this. And she
never will."

Now, Sir, I am one of those who " entirely trust "
Mr. Parnell, in Mr. Bright's sense, and I took note of
his sneer at Scotland for its perfect consistency with
aspirations for the severance of the last link which
binds Ireland to Great Britain.

I am, Sir, your obedient servant,

March 21.   M.P.

[*" Times" Supplement, March* 25, 1887.]

To the Editor of the " Times."

Sir,—Sir John Lubbock will, I hope, permit me to
say that he awards to himself an easy victory over
an imaginary foe. I know of no person of any
authority who has ever argued for " separate

Legislatures for England, Scotland, Ireland, and Wales on the basis of the existence of four distinct races occupying these four geographical regions." The idea is fantastic. What my letter of last Monday did was to point out that Sir J. Lubbock had mistaken the point of Mr. Gladstone's remark by hastily assuming that " race " and " nationality " are synonymous. They are entirely different. You may have different nationalities of a race practically the same. You may have a nationality composed of several races. So far therefore from admitting Sir J. Lubbock's contention, I have shown that his contention is based on a misconception, and does not touch Mr. Gladstone's real argument. As his second letter does not touch it either, it need not be repeated by me.

With regard to the minor historical points of both his letters, I frankly admit that statements in support of which respectable, even if old-fashioned, authorities can be cited ought not to be called " inaccuracies," and I willingly withdraw any expression which can cause annoyance to a friend who, even in controversy, is fair and courteous. These points, as your article observes, are of no consequence to the present discussion, because I agree with him that the population of Scotland is composed of diverse elements, and have stated the fact more broadly than he did. But I must repeat my dissent from his details. As regards one of them, he mistakes my contradiction. Everybody knows that the name of Sutherland is, like Caithness, a name given by the Norsemen, but that proves nothing as to the population, which is overwhelmingly Celtic. London and Dover are Celtic names, but what does that prove as to their population ? He practically admits my correction as to the Bruces; and the writers he refers to on the other points are not, except Mr. Skene, such as modern students will deem weighty. Alex. Chalmers was a good antiquary for his time, but the very quotation Sir J. Lubbock makes from him about Britons and Saxons indicates, to those who have followed recent discussions, how much has been done since his day to clear up the ethnology of early Britain. But I must not occupy your space with inquiries and citations of counter-authorities fitter for the *Historical Review* than for the columns of a daily journal ; and I leave the subject by reiterating (what, indeed, your article has said) that questions relating to the original elements of the population of our islands shed so little light upon our present problem that to drag them into it is to make confusion worse confounded. . We might as well inquire whether Lord

Edward Fitzgerald, Archibald Hamilton Rowan, and Mr. Parnell himself ought to be reckoned Nationalists, seeing that their families came from Great Britain.

But at the end of his letter Sir J. Lubbock starts a new hare. He seems to attribute to me an opinion regarding Ireland which I have never held nor expressed, and which is no part either of Mr. Gladstone's argument or of my own. I have never said, no English Home Ruler known to me has said, that Ireland is at present a cohesive whole. What we do say, and what the history of the last 110 years amply proves, is that there exists a passionate feeling of nationality among the great bulk of the Irish people, a feeling which has resisted all the attempts of England to ignore or to extinguish it. It was just as strong among the Protestant patriots of 1782 and the Protestant insurgents of Ulster in 1798 as it is among the Nationalists of 1887. It is not a matter of race or religion only, for it is now shared by many Protestants and many descendants of Englishmen and Scotchmen. We hold that it is the unwise policy of England that has forced this feeling into antagonism to what the Irish masses call "the English Government." Had Scotland been dealt with as Ireland has been, the

E

national sentiment of Scotland might have been driven into the same hostility.   Had the Scottish policy of James II. been continued by William and Anne and the Georges, had the Union of 1707 been carried as a part of that policy, would Scotland have been any more loyal to the Act of 1707 than Ireland has been to the Act of 1800 ?   If Ireland had received, even after 1800, the same treatment which Scotland has generally received since 1689, O'Connell would never have raised the standard of repeal.

I well remember Mr. Parnell's speech in 1885, to which your anonymous correspondent " M.P." (who might with advantage imitate Sir J. Lubbock's courtesy) refers.   I remember the amused astonishment with which Scotchmen received it.   Scotland has not parted with her nationality or become merged in England.   By her acceptance of the wider nationality of the United Kingdom and of the English-speaking race throughout the world, she has not lost her proper national feeling, her attachment to her own law, to her own form of Christianity, to her own historic memories and institutions.   She does not honour William Wallace and John Knox the less because she can now also claim a share in Simon of Montfort and John Hampden.   Satisfied in the main with her own

government, which is administered by persons
whom she trusts, and with her own laws, which are
generally conformable to her wishes (though she
complains that the Imperial Parliament gives her far
too little of its time), she does not ask for, because she
does not need, the same changes in her relation to
England as the vast majority of the Irish people now
demand for themselves. Irish history has been so
different from Scottish, that it would be strange
indeed if the same measures of reform were required
for both the countries.

When, therefore, we are reminded of the contrast
between the attitude of Scotland and that of Ireland
our answer is twofold. Scotland is contented because
she has received justice and equality, because she has
practically been allowed to manage her own affairs.
Why should not justice, equality, and the sense of
responsibility bear their appropriate fruits in Ireland
also ?

Scotland, which so late as 1745 was a divided
country, and whose national feeling was once bitterly
hostile to England, is now a united country, and
cherishes a local patriotism which strengthens instead
of clashing with her Imperial patriotism. Why should
not the same come to pass in Ireland also when the

springs of discontent and resentment have been dried up by a wise and generous policy ?

Your faithful servant,

March 25.   J. BRYCE.

[" *Times*," *March* 28, 1887.]

To the Editor of the "Times."

Sir,—Mr. Bryce, in his reply to Sir John Lubbock, speaks in a somewhat *ex cathedrâ* manner of Sir John's "minor inaccuracies," which he proceeds to point out.

These so-called inaccuracies are all, however, either simple facts, or statements of opinion, based on authority, on matters not susceptible of complete proof.

Thus it is true that the Saxons were in Scotland a little before the Scots, *i.e.*, that the Northumbrians occupied the country about the Lower Tweed before the Dalriadic Scots effected a permanent settlement in Argyle. Celtic philologists seldom agree about etymologies ; but that which Sir John Lubbock gives for the word "Argyle," though not the only one in the field, is the one generally accepted. The names

Cambrun and Camburn occur in the Ragman Roll,
and their owners were probably the ancestors of the
Lowland Camerons, if not of the chiefs of the
Highland clan. Sir John did not, as I read him,
positively assert that there was very much Scandinavian
blood in Sutherland ; but he might have done so with
safety : the people of Western Sutherland exhibit
unmistakable signs of Scandinavianism in their
physique as well as in clan and place-names. The
Kennedys were derived by Nisbet from Ireland ; and
the Munroes have a tradition that they came from
Ulster. That the Bruces were directly or indirectly
of Norwegian origin we are all agreed, and it makes
in Sir John's favour ; while the pedigree of Sir William
Wallace, as given by the author of " The Norman
People," brings his family to Scotland from the borders
of Shropshire.

Yours, &c.,

CLIFTON, *March* 23.   JOHN BEDDOE.

[" *Times,*" *March* , 1887.]

TO THE EDITOR OF THE " TIMES."

SIR,—Sir John Lubbock is unquestionably right
when he asserts the identity of the people of Ireland

and the people of Great Britain, as regards their
common origin in a mixture of the same races. There is
absolutely no distinction between them in this respect.
We are all mongrels, and not only are we all equally
mongrels, but we are the result of the intermixture of
precisely the same breeds all over the United Kingdom.
In examining lately the earliest history of Scotland, I
have been much struck by the comparative lateness of
the period down to which the constituent races were
still so separate as to be separately named and
enumerated in the language of authority. During the
two centuries and more which elapsed between the
Norman conquest of England and the war of Scottish
independence, there were in Scotland four, if not five,
"well-marked nationalities." They were sometimes
separately addressed in Royal proclamations and in
other public documents as Scots, Angles, French
(Normans), and Galwegians. Of these, two were
Celtic of different branches, the Scots and Galwegians,
and two were Teutonic, while a fifth element of great
power, the Scandinavian, was predominant in the
north and west. It was the work—the glorious and
civilising work—of our best kings to effect the welding
and amalgamation of these separate nationalities into
one. It is now the barbarous work of the Parnellite

Liberals to undo the work of union all over the three kingdoms, and to sunder the "goodly fellowship" which had been established by greater men and in happier times.   Why is it that no Englishman thinks or speaks with reluctance of the Conquest?   It is because he is conscious of that ancient union which makes him a representative both of those who conquered and of those who were subdued.   Sir John Lubbock does good service when he reminds all Irishmen that they are in precisely the same position.   It is true that the processes of amalgamation in Ireland were less happy, but, so far as the mixture and inheritance of common blood are concerned, those processes were not less complete.   The proudest names in the history of Ireland are names representing a perfect union of the races.   Not a few of the most devoted adherents of each and of all the political parties into which Ireland has been unhappily divided have borne indifferently names of Celtic and of Norman origin, and at the present moment many of those whom the Parnellite faction desire to expropriate and banish from Ireland are, and have been for 700 years, "more Irish than the Irish."   The language of party leaders who dare to speak of these men as unpatriotic because they refuse to sacrifice the Union at the bidding of faction, is thoroughly characteristic of the unscrupulous and fanatical spirit in which the whole movement is conducted.

But, besides the absence of any dividing line between us and the Irish people in respect to race, there is also a complete absence of any historical separation between them in respect to those other elements which sometimes contribute to establish the national distinctions.   There may be real separate nationalities among people of the same race.   Widely separated geographical positions, distinct, definite, and continuous growths of law and government, may establish, and may even of necessity constitute, such separate nationalities.   Can this be truly said of Ireland as distinguished from Great Britain?   Let us hear the voice of an Irish historian—animated with almost a fierce spirit of antagonism to those he calls "the English"—Mr. Prendergast, author of the "Cromwellian Settlement of Ireland."   In condemning the language, born of local and temporary contests, which used to designate insurgent septs as the "Irish enemy," Mr. Prendergast uses these remarkable words :—

"Now, the 'Irish enemy' was no nation in the modern sense of the word, but a race divided into many nations or tribes, separately defending their lands from the English barons in their immediate neighbourhood. There has been no ancient national government displaced—no national dynasty overthrown ; the Irish had no national flag, nor any capital city as the metropolis of their common country, nor any common administration of law ; nor did they ever give a combined opposition to the English. The English, coming in the name of the Pope, with the aid of the Irish Bishops, and with a superior national organisation, which the Irish easily recognised, were accepted by the Irish. Neither King Henry II. nor King John ever fought a battle in Ireland."

Again, a few pages further on, the same author says :—

" The Irish gave no national resistance to the English ; they had no dynasty to set up; no common government to restore ; no national capital to recover." (Pages 28 and 30.)

These statements, remarkable in themselves, and still more remarkable coming from such a source, are not only strictly true, but they are far within the truth —by which I mean that they do not nearly exhaust the facts which establish the same conclusions. The " superior national organisation," which the Irish " easily recognised," consisted in a system of law and of jurisprudence, and it was the great sin and blunder of the English for a long time that they excluded the native Irish from its benefits, which they were anxious to secure and to enjoy. It can be shown beyond question that most of the miseries of the Irish people have arisen from the long survival of some ancient native usages and habits, and from the grudging and reluctant application to the Irish of that higher organ- isation to which they ought to have been admitted universally and at once.   Complete union and amal- gamation on perfectly equal terms with the noblest Empire in the world was the natural issue and the right consummation of all the facts.   This is what Mr. Pitt intended to offer.   This is what we should endeavour to complete ; and it is this which we need never be ashamed to defend.

March 26.   ARGYLL.

[" *Times*," *March* 31, 1887.]

To the Editor of the "Times."

Sir,— There was unquestionably a very widely entertained idea that, when the existence of " real nationalities " was adduced as an argument in favour of Home Rule, it was implied that there were different races of men in England, Scotland, Ireland, and Wales respectively.   If indeed the argument does not mean this, it seems to have very little meaning at all, and my first letter has effected its object in clearing up this point.

Professor Bryce sneers at the authorities I cited. I will only say that, writing in the library of the House of Commons, I quoted the writers selected by our worthy librarian, who would, no doubt, be prepared to defend them if necessary.

As a Unionist, I have read the latter part of Professor Bryce's letter with both surprise and pleasure. He says that Scotland, which " so late as 1745 was a divided country, and whose national feeling was once bitterly hostile to England, is now a united country, and cherishes a local patriotism which strengthens instead of clashing with her Imperial patriotism. Why should not the same come to pass in Ireland also, when the springs of discontent and resentment have been dried up by a wise and generous policy?" Why not, indeed? But, Sir, we did not then yield to this " bitterly hostile" feeling in Scotland; we did not constitute separate Legislatures in 1745 ; our forefathers maintained the union with Scotland then, as, if we are true to ourselves, we shall maintain the union with Ireland now. From economic causes Ireland has suffered much in recent years, but we hope that better times may now be in store for her; and, as England and Scotland have " accepted the wider nationality of the United Kingdom," so I ask, in the words of Professor Bryce himself, "why should not the same come to pass in Ireland also, when the springs of discontent and resentment have been dried up by a wise and generous policy?"

I am, Sir, your obedient servant,

JOHN LUBBOCK.

HOUSE OF COMMONS, *March* 28.

[" *Times*," *March* 31, 1887.]

————

TO THE EDITOR OF THE " TIMES."

SIR,—Sir John Lubbock's third letter requires only a very few words in reply.

As he cites no passage in which Mr. Gladstone or any other Liberal has maintained the strange notion against which his first letter was directed, it may, I think, be assumed that he withdraws the charge it contained, and that he admits that race and nationality are different things.

The reason he gives for not citing weightier authorities needs no comment. If I understand aright his reference to Scotland, it rests on a misconception of the events of 1745. His argument seems to assume that the rebellion of that year was an effort of the Scottish nation to shake off the union with England. It was nothing of the kind. It was essentially a rebellion of Highland chiefs with some Lowland Jacobites, nearly all Episcopalians. As Sir Walter Scott says, "by far the greater part of Scotland was attached to the House of Hanover and to the principles which placed them on the throne." Neither at nor after 1745 did England refuse any demand of the Scottish people for an alteration in the relations of the countries, for no such demand was made.

It is pleasant to find, at the end of this controversy, that Sir J. Lubbock does not deny that the difference between the attitude of Scotland and of Ireland may be attributed to the different way in which the two countries and their respective national feelings have been dealt with, and that he joins in the hope I have ventured to express as to the results of a wise and generous policy towards Ireland. One cannot but hope further that he and others equally fair-minded will join in opposing a measure in which few signs of generosity can be discerned, and in demanding other measures more likely to implant in the Irish people that attachment to the United Kingdom which Scotland displays.

I am your faithful servant,

House of Commons, *March* 31.   J. BRYCE.

[*"Times," April* 2, 1887.]

To the Editor of the "Times."

Sir,—Will you allow me space once more for a few words, in reply to Professor Bryce.

In the first place, I see no reason to retract anything I have said ; and, secondly, I did not give a " reason for not citing weightier authorities." On the contrary, I gave my reason for considering that the authorities were weighty.

But, what is of more importance, Professor Bryce says that I do " not deny that the differences between the attitude of Scotland and of Ireland may be attributed to the different way in which the two countries and their national feelings have been dealt with." If Professor Bryce means that this is the main cause, I must entirely demur.   I have admitted nothing of the kind.

My contention, on the contrary, has always been that the discontent in Ireland is mainly due to the sufferings which the people have undergone from the partial failure of the potato, the fall in agricultural prices, and other economical causes. " Before the Irish famine," says Sir Lyon Playfair, " the average produce of potatoes in Ireland was between six and seven tons per acre, but it then fell to three and a quarter tons per acre, or to less than one-half ; and in other crops the same melancholy reduction of produce has occurred." Under these circumstances, her population, which had risen between 1800 and 1840 from 5,000,000 to over 8,000,000, has dwindled, from circumstances over which we had no control, down again to about 5,000,000. This implies great misery, and if we sometimes think our Irish fellow-countrymen unjust and unreasonable, we must remember how terribly they have suffered, and that under such circumstances no Government could be popular.

We may, however, I think, fairly hope that the present population is one which the country can maintain in reasonable comfort, and that with happier times a happier feeling will arise. It is, moreover, I believe, the opinion of the vast majority of men of business that Ireland has a better chance of material prosperity if the Union is maintained intact than if it be in any way weakened ; and I do not think that under such circumstances we should be justified in giving way to the present desire for a separate Parliament, more especially as it is strenuously opposed by so large and intelligent a minority in Ireland itself.

I am your obedient servant,

JOHN LUBBOCK.

33, BELGRAVE SQUARE, S.W., *April* 7.
["*Times*," *April* 9, 1887.]

TO THE EDITOR OF THE "TIMES."

SIR,—Let us accept Mr. Bryce's idea of nationalities. According to him they are independent of race, language, &c., and are based, in short, on the mere sentiment of national union.

No one such sentiment imbues all Ireland. If we admit the existence there of one, which is anti-British, disloyal, separatist, we cannot shut our eyes to that of another, which is loyal and Imperialistic, dominating, it may be, a minority of the population, but a larger part of the intellect, energy, and wealth of the country. And it is this second nationality which Mr. Bryce and his friends would induce us to abandon in the faint hope of conciliating the first.

Yours obediently,

CLIFTON, *April* 3.   JOHN BEDDOE.
["*Times*," *April* 9, 1887.]

To Sir John Lubbock.

My dear Lubbock,—I have read your letter with interest, and, as against Bryce, I certainly concur with you.

At the same time I think both you and the Duke of Argyll tend to minimise the Celtic predominance in certain districts. Whether the Saxons were in Caledonia before the Scots or not, the Scots were only a section of the Goidhelic Celts, who certainly occupied Scotland before the arrival of the Teutons.

We Maxwells trace our descent from Maccus, a Manx pirate, probably a Norseman; one of the eight sub-kings who are said to have rowed King Edgar on the Dee. He appears on a grant by King Edgar to the monastery of Glastonbury, on which he describes himself as " Arch-pirate." The signatures are in the following order:—

Ego + Edgar rex tocius Britanniæ,
 ,, ,, Eggifa ejusdem regis mater,
 ,, ,, Edward (his son),
 ,, ,, Kynadius rex Albaniæ,
 ,, ,, Mascusius Archipirata,
 ,, ,, Dunstanus Dorobernensis Eccl. Archi-
            episcopus,
 ,, ,, Oswald Eboracensis Eccl. primus,

G

and so on. The appearance of the Arch-pirate between the King and the Archbishop is very curious! The present form of our name is territorial, derived from Maccus well, a pool in the Tweed, now called Maxwheel.

Yours truly,

HERBERT EUSTACE MAXWELL.

HOUSE OF COMMONS, *March* 31, 1887.

MY DEAR LUBBOCK,—I am glad to have had the opportunity of perusing, as a whole, the correspondence in which you have been engaged respecting the nationalities included within the, as yet, United Kingdom of Great Britain and Ireland.

It particularly interests me to observe that the plea for dealing with the inhabitants of Ireland on political and moral principles inconsistent with those which are accepted in Scotland and England, on the ground of a supposed difference of race, appears to be abandoned. I remember when it was in high favour. The desire to possess yourself of your neighbour's land was admitted to be a breach of the tenth commandment in Great Britain ; but in Ireland such craving was "earth-hunger"—a sort of natural and commendable appetite innate in the "Celt," and confounded with dishonesty only by the gross and unpoetic nature of the Saxon.

So long ago as 1870, I brought a great storm upon my head by a lecture on the "Forefathers and Forerunners of the English People," in which I ventured to point out that, even if we make the serious and questionable admission that the principles of morality and polity are different for Celtic from what they are for Teutonic races, that wonderful doctrine can have no more application in any one of the three kingdoms than in another.

For, as you have well urged, we have as good evidence as can possibly be attained on such questions, that the same elements have entered into the composition of the population in England, Scotland, and Ireland ; and that the ethnic differences between the three lie simply in the general and local proportions of these elements in each region. I asserted, in 1870, that the population of Cornwall and Devon has as much claim to the title of "Celtic" as that of Tipperary. The statement was hotly repudiated on both the English and the Irish sides ; but, in my judgment, its accuracy remains unaffected.

I believe I should be justified in extending it to a

very much larger area—certainly to north-west England and south-west Scotland.

It really is a great comfort to find that scientific truth makes its way, however slowly ; and that when a statesman speaks of the existence of four "real nationalities" in these islands, he does not mean to revive the exploded fallacies about Celt and Teuton which were current and did endless mischief a score of years ago. And it must be an equally great comfort to those who accept this loose talk about "four nationalities" that they have got out of the grip of Science, and can avail themselves of the popular connotation of a phraseology which is not susceptible of clear definition.

Undoubtedly there are four geographical regions, England, Scotland, Wales, and Ireland, and the people who live in them call themselves and are called by others the English, Scotch, Welsh, and Irish nations. It is also true that the inhabitants of the Isle of Man call themselves Manxmen, and are just as proud of their nationality as any other "nationalities." I am not sure that the Orcadians would be quite content to merge themselves altogether in the Scottish nationality. And there is, at any rate, one Hebridean isle whose pastor used to pray for "the people of the adjacent island of Great Britain," and who, therefore, would seem to have considered his own people a distinct " nationality."

We may admit the existence of all these nationalities or groups of people, more or less individualised by geographical or historical circumstances ; and, indeed, the list might be plausibly extended. But if we mean no more than this by " nationality," the term has no practical significance. If we do mean more, then we must ascribe to such nationalities either ethnological or historical individuality. The Irish " nationality " is no more an ethnological individuality than the English or the Scotch ; and as to historical individuality, Ireland has, unhappily, been a house divided against itself, from the earliest ages to the present day. When the inhabitants of Ireland constitute a " nationality " in the sense that the term applies to those of England, Scotland, and Wales, it will be possible to speak of the " four nationalities " of our common country, without deluding ourselves and others.

I am yours very faithfully,

T. H. HUXLEY.

May 2, 1887.

GYFLA.

THE SCÍR OR *PAGUS* OF THE IVEL VALLEY, SOMERSET.

BY THOMAS KERSLAKE.

A VERY early catalogue of above thirty Anglo-Saxon settlements in the southern half of this island has long engaged the attention of our political antiquaries. It consists entirely of Teutonic names, or of names which had already fallen into Teutonic forms or usage ; but it shares with the earlier Celtic list of British cities, usually printed with Nennius, in that, whilst the majority of the names in both are the merest riddles as to what places are meant, a small number in each can be fairly guessed, and a few can be positively recognised.

This Anglo-Saxon list has been several times printed, from more or less corrupted copies ; by Sir Henry Spelman in his "Glossarium"[*]; in Gale and Fell's "Scriptores"[†]; and by Mr. Kemble.[‡] But a much earlier and evidently a more accurate copy

---

[*] Voc. Hida. [†] Vol. III. p. 743.
[‡] "Saxons in England," I. 81.

was lately discovered by Mr. W. De Gray Birch, and printed in his "Cartularium Saxonicum"[*]; also supplemented by an exposition, attempting to localise the names, in the Journal of the British Archæological Association.[†] Mr. Birch attributes the writing of this copy to the tenth or eleventh century, but justly considers it to represent a document of an earlier date, and we shall presently see an additional reason to consider it to have been derived from a record of the early part of the eighth century, by an example of what must have been the condition at that time of one of the territories mentioned, to qualify it for a place in such a contemporary catalogue.

Among the names in this Teutonic list is one which can not only be recognised with certainty, but of which, I believe, I am able to fairly indicate the extent of the district intended. This is "Gifla," numbered 15 by Mr. Birch. Spelman prints it "Eyfla." Gale and Fell print "Cifla," but suggest "Gyfla," but they all confess no knowledge of the place meant. Mr. Kemble prints "Eysla," but three other manuscripts printed by Mr. Birch read "Gyfla," which is no doubt the true reading. The name had already otherwise been well known as "Gifle," from that Gazetteer of old Wessex Topography, King Alfred's Will; but this both Mr. Kemble and Mr. Thorp had perversely explained as "Gidley," and so the real rendering had been hitherto diverted and lost from general knowledge.

Mr. Birch, however, comes nearer home when he suggests "Yeovil," but when he goes on to call it "the supposed Roman Station *Velox*," he seems rather to have meant the town of Ilchester or Ivelchester, and we shall see that it does mean a large pagus, or tract of country, in which both these places are situated. In either case, he appears to forget that this Teutonic list is not, like the older Celtic one, a list of cities or towns, but of districts. Sir H. Spelman calls them "regiunculæ." Mr. Kemble includes the list in his chapter "The Gá or Scír." This word, "Gá," is probably one of Mr. Kemble's German importations. The only resting-place for this word in any English record is this very Saxon list; on the ground that six of the names therein contained end with "ga." But there is no reason to value this as a significant annexed word at all, but simply an ordinary termination, Fifteen other of the names end in "na." All end in "a." So that all that is peculiar to the six that end in "ga" is that "g" happens to be the

H

penultimate letter, which is "n" in fifteen other names, and other consonants in the rest.

If, however, we had found the other word "Scir" in any title or rubric of this Anglo-Saxon list, we need not have been surprised; for this word would have been at home in an English record. But, even with respect to this word, it has been contended that our word "shire" is distinctive of those English counties that had not been original territories or "regiunculæ," afterwards constituents of larger territories or kingdoms, but that it indicates later divisions or *shares* of such larger territories that had been already established or consolidated. Long before our con stitution of shires, as an administrative sub-division of an already consolidated kingdom, there is reason to believe that "scirs" had a different and independent existence. Shearings off they may have been, but from the possessions of the invaded Celtic peoples : colonies, conquests, or encroachments; not always even hostile, though afterwards aggregated by the advance of the Anglo-Saxon aggressive central powers, incited by the imperial instinct. Hallamshire and Hexhamshire are among many examples of the survival in local usage of the names of some territorial arrangements older than our divisions of a greater centralisation into our shires. Another example is the name "Triconscir" in King Alfred's will. In the most authentic printed books this has always been interpreted as meaning "Cornwall" at large, but it only means that part or "scir" of Cornwall which had been inherited by Alfred, and of which the name still remains, in a reduced form, in the name of the two hundreds of "Trigg." It is remarkable that this is the very part of Cornwall which had long been exceptionally English, having, as I have elsewhere shown,* been already *sheared* off from Celtic Damnonia by Æthelbald of Mercia, A.D. 743 : and this perhaps accounts for Alfred's possession of it, by heritage under his West-Saxon absorption of the territories and royalties of Mercia.

If, indeed, the circumstances of this Cornish " Triconscir," or " Trigg," should be looked at a little nearer, it is thought that it will offer a strong confirmation of the above suggestion, that "scir" originally signified a shearing off or annexation of territory from that of our Celtic forefathers, by those of the Teutonic or sinister field of our pedigree. Although Triconscir has survived to us in the name of

* "Vestiges of the Supremacy of Mercia," 1879, 15-19 (Bristol and Glouc. Trans., vol. III., pp. 119, &c.).

Trigg, it did not so survive as the name of the two hundreds as it has since become. The name, no doubt, continued to live in the ecclesiastical division of the deaneries of Trigg Minor and Major, which still retained the name as " Trigris*schir*," A.D. 1291-2.* These two deaneries occupy the whole of the north-eastern angle of Cornwall, with the coast of the Severn Sea all the way to the obvious western natural frontier of the estuary of the Camel. These ecclesiastical divisions, still called Trigg, extend over the three present civil hundreds, of Trigg, Lesnewth, and Stratton. But these three civil hundreds, although they were already divided, A.D. 1402-3,† must have had a later, or at least a separate and independent cause.

So much for Triconscir and its descent to our time. But this district is very exactly continued to the south coast in two other deaneries, which are also hundreds, now known by the naked names of " East" and " West." But these two names are only the outlying prefixes of the ancient names of these two deaneries : " Estwel*shire* " and " Westwell*chir*,"‡ of which a second manuscript reads, " Estwewel*sire* " and

* Taxatio P. Nic. IV. pp. 148-154.
† 3rd of Henry IV., Carew's Survey, foll. 39-42.
‡ Taxatio P. Nic. IV.

" Westwewil*chir*," and called by Carew* "West-wibil*sher*" and " Eastwibil*shere.*" This southern continuation has for its natural frontiers the estuary of Fowey, the English Channel, and Plymouth Sound. Here then we have plainly—not in present usage, but within the safe reach of our inquiry,—the word *"shire"* attached to the whole of a march district from sea to sea, semi-annexed or shorn off from our Celtic county.

At all events, the list under our attention is a record of this sort of "scirs," or insulated colonies or first settlements, of the Teutonic invaders or immigrants, among the hitherto partially subjugated Britons. Our immediate concern is with the one, of its recorded districts before mentioned, which appears as "Gifla" in the more ancient copy ; and it is here selected for notice because it is believed that the first Saxon occupation of the territory so named can be actually dated : A.D. 658.

In the Anglo-Saxon Chronicle is this Annal :—

" An. DCLVIII. In this year Cenwalh (or Kenwalch) fought æt Poennum with the Wealas (Damnonian Britons), and made them fly as far as Pedrida (the river Parret)."

All preceding writers who have attempted to place

* Carew, foll. 92-93.

the " Peon " here mentioned have at once jumped at
a guess at some one of the many places which have
retained the Celtic name of " Pen." But it is most
unlikely that the Saxons should have converted this
short *e* into a diphthong. They were not in the habit
so to treat the British " Pen " in names wherein they
found and adopted it. They also had more substantial
uses for diphthongs than to waste them where they
were not due. I have already, in a treatise formerly
under the notice of this Society,* shown good reasons,
now somewhat strengthened by this mention of the
district of Gyfla among the Saxon colonies, that the
" Peon " of the battle was Poinington Down, north of
Sherborne, the last natural fastness, westward, of the
high range of hills that divides our Dorset, already
occupied by the West-Saxon invaders for a hundred
years, and our Somerset, which by this battle they
penetrated for the first time. This eminence looks
down, westward, upon the extensive valley through
which flows the river Yeovil, Ivel, or Yeo, and
including the towns of Yeovil, of Ivelchester,
Yeovilton, and one or two other places in which the
river-name may be traced. But near the mouth of
the valley the river Yeo joins the river Parret near

* " A Primæval British Metropolis," pp. 45-64. Once discussed
on the field by the Somerset Society.

Langport; so that the fugitives here first encountered that river, and it is here that the pursuit was checked, and that day converted the district of the Yeo valley, from a British possession, to the West-Saxon colony of " Gyfla."

The flight and pursuit must have been for about twelve or fifteen miles, and the valley in which the pursuers now found themselves is one of those which are so characteristic of Somerset: a long and broad alluvial level, or drained estuary or frith, confined by semi-mountainous ranges of hills, admirably suited to such an intended colony. Having expelled the occupants, the continued occupation of such a region was the obvious sequel. Not only was the capacious basin in which they found themselves all that could be desired, but any of you who may now make the short journey from Yeovil to Sherborne, even by the present capital oblique road, may have some experience of the greater difficulty of the retreat than what the precipitate advance had been. At the eastern end of the basin, the steep western escarpment is crowned by the plain which had been the battle-field ; at the western extremity was the contingency of the Parret, to which the Chronicle assigns the cessation of the pursuit. I will not here enter upon the proof of the enormous errors of ethnology and history, that have been repeated from each other, until they have become textual, by all established writers, and which arose out of a wrong understanding of this mention of the river Parret. I have to some extent done this in the treatise already referred to.[*]

It has been said above that, by this conquest of A.D. 658, Somerset was "penetrated for the first time." It is indeed the first Teutonic occupancy of any part of Somerset proper. It is true the earlier conquest of the Gloucestershire Cotswolds by Ceawlin, A.D. 577, included Bath ; and as Bath is placed in Somersetshire in modern Gazetteers, even the older school of "best authorities," such for instance as Mr. Sharon Turner, had, for the sake of the turn of a sentence, included "a part of Somerset" in that conquest. The late learned and ingenious Dr. Edwin Guest, without any warrant or justification from the original authority, the annal in the Chronicle, or any other, extended the conquest, spite of the Avon, of Wansdike, and the mountain-group of the Mendips, beyond all these formidable barriers and impediments, to include the part, probably about one-third of the present county, which lies north of the small north Somerset Axe ; and his

* "A Primæval British Metropolis," p. 62.

premature extension has since passed without question into all the received histories of England. But the conquest on the Gloucestershire Cotswold range had only for an incidental result the pillage of the three Roman cities—Bath, Cirencester, and Gloucester, —which lay at three of its feet, and does not indicate any extent of the territorial annexations that were then realised. But that Bath, which is, alone by itself, north of the Avon, and always racially distinct from the south of the river, is included in the Somerset of our day is an accident probably arising in the eleventh century out of changes in Church territory, and in direct disregard of both natural and ethnic frontier.

I have shown in the treatise last cited that this north part of Somerset has distinct traces of a late continuance of Celtic Christianity, and your own Society lately produced another striking one, that the alias of "Lantocai," for Leigh-upon-Mendip, is still in use. There are several names of British Saints quite likely to have passed into "Tocai," but the prefix "Lan-" is at any rate an indisputable mark.

There are also similar indications that Dr. Guest has exceeded his authorities in extending the Cotswold conquest westward, to the angle of Gloucestershire

I

that lies between the Severn and the Avon. This is a quite separate high range of limestone table-land, divided from the Cotswolds by the wide forest bottom, since known as Kingswood Forest. In the times concerned a forest must have been one of the most effectual of natural checks to an invader. Every tree must have been a fortress, even when garrisoned by only one or two defenders. This part of Gloucestershire must have continued Celtic until included in the advance of Mercia to the Avon against Wessex, above a hundred years later. Of the late Celtic occupation of this region, besides some hagiographical traces in dedications, the charters of Worcester show the Mercians dealing with the whole of it as conquerors deal with newly-appropriated lands ; and some of these charters of this eastern shore are remarkable examples of the peculiar rentals in kind which have been noticed by Mr. Seebohm at Tidenham, on the opposite Welsh or western side of the Severn.

Just beyond the confluence of the Yeo with the Parret is the Isle of Athelney, which, not until more than two hundred years later than the time upon which we have been engaged, earned its greater renown under King Alfred. Cenwalch has the reputation of having founded Sherborne Monastery close to Poinington, where the battle had been fought. There is also some reason to suspect that he founded a religious college of some sort at Athelney, where the conquest ended, since forgotten by eclipse of later events. William of Malmesbury* superciliously notes that, even as late as the twelfth century, there were a few poor monks at Athelney who still continued to sing to the stars the praises of St. Eielwin, their patron, whose still-continued endowments they counted instead of sanctity: and that it was believed that he was the brother of Cenwalch. Was Eielwin the Atheling of Athelinga-ey? Alfred found the name already there; so the name cannot have arisen from his own Athelings.

The realising of the date of the settlement of an English people in a particular locality may have other subordinate points of importance. For example, within this region of Gyfla is a place the name of which includes the constituent "-ing," about which Mr. Seebohm says the last word has not yet been said. This sort of historical contribution may therefore be valuable even to the positivisms of philology, for within this colony is a " Lym*ing*ton," of which a most

---

* "Gesta Pontificum," Rolls edn., p. 199.

learned etymologist* lately said, "As to Lymington, it is a town of Lymings, a tribe also commemorated by the village of Lyminge in Kent." For this to be true it would be necessary that this tribe should have been common to the Jutish settlers of the fifth century, and the Gewissæ of the seventh. I have already contended† that the "-ing" of English names is most often an adaptation of the Celtic "ynys" or "inch," found already on any spot so named, as being a river island, or peninsular shore ; and I think Lymington on the Ivel fairly satisfies this condition. Lymington is the place where Wolsey is said to have sown his wild oats, and to have consequently watched his vigil in the "enchanted castle" of Sir Hudibras. This Yeo valley also produced another celebrity—Thomas Coryat, "the Odcombian leg-stretcher," who walked nearly two thousand miles through Europe with a single pair of shoes. The shoes were said to have been hung as a memorial trophy in the Church of Odcombe. I once performed a "leg-stretching" pilgrimage to that fane, but failed to see or hear of the shoes. In Coryat's work, Yeovil is usually called "Evil."

14, WEST PARK, BRISTOL.

* *Notes and Queries*, April 21st, 1883.
† *Notes and Queries*, 6th S. VIII. 113.

LONDON, 15, PICCADILLY,

March 23, 1887.

MY DEAR MR. KERSLAKE,

I am always glad to hear from you.

Your antiquarian researches are so very similar to mine, that I quite envy your ability to follow up our hobby, while I remain a slave to business.

In your pamphlet "Gyfla" you call the Teutonic element in the English race the *sinister* one ! I differ with you there *in toto.* Read Sir John Lubbock's letter in the *Times* Supplement of March 19, headed " Mr. Gladstone and the Nationalities of the United Kingdom." I recognise only Imperial interests, and as long as the Celt is loyal he is a dear brother to me. When he is disloyal, then I am in favour of fire and sword. I would stamp out disloyalty with an iron heel.

On page 9 you want to change the Teutonic ending "-ing" into a Celtic one ! No, my dear Mr. Kerslake; do not let your enthusiasm blind you. " Lyminge " and such-like names ending with *ing* and *ung* belong to

Teutonic nomenclature.   You know the " Islend*inga*"
Saga, and the " Niebel*ungen* Lied."

With best wishes for your health,

I ever remain, my dear friend,

Yours sincerely,

BERNARD QUARITCH.

Dear Mr. Quaritch,

I thank you for your kind and interesting
letter.   I thought it was obvious that I had used the
word   " sinister "   in its heraldic sense, wherein it
means the later accession to the family coat, and most
generally the "better half."   In this western part of
England we are much more Celtic in race than
Teutonic.   I do not know that we are the better for
it, but the sound of the name of " Briton " echoed
back from the other ends of the world has a pleasant
ring upon our ears.   Our Raleigh, our Drake, our
Hooker, Roger Bacon, Blake, Marlborough, Locke,
Cudworth, and many of their fellows, were more
Celtic than if they had been born in Dublin or Cork
or Waterford, *Hilernis Celtiores*.   Our St. Boniface
Archbishop of Mainz, had his Christianity, of which

he planted the hierarchy in Germany, from his Celtic Damnonian mother, in spite of his pagan Teutonic father. Of course, I must concede to you the present condition of Ireland, whatever it amounts to. But of the earlier times with which we were dealing there are some *ad hominem* considerations (excuse them), such as the wonderful cover of the Book of Kells. I have said more about the "-ing" question on a former occasion,* and do not see reason to retract. I happen to have observed some of the places. I do not claim all the "-ings." Indeed, generalisations in these matters are often mistaken and mischievous. Causes and their results are much mixed in these and all other things. I have found myself not the only one who cannot digest Mr. Kemble's 1,300 -ings.

I thank you for your three catalogues. I have often wished to see them. The time is now passed when I can do anything with them. I did, however, see one lot in the MSS. which might be worth your while to bring to the notice of Jonathan Rashleigh, Esq., Menabilly, Par Station, Cornwall. It is No. 35,799, Cornwall, on page 3,501. What wonderful high numbers!

I have not been seeing the *Times* lately. I have,

* *Notes and Queries*, April 21, 1883.

however, ordered the 19th.   The present Irish are suffering from a bad education, including their latest under a vacillating, obsequious, and dangerous states- man.   A small action of a firm hand four or five years ago would have saved much evil since and present danger.

I am proud of your constant triumphs, and wish you long continuance and health.   What more of a " hobby " do you want than the opportunity, free from impertinent editing, furnished by your own catalogues ?

Yours very truly,

THOMAS KERSLAKE.

14, WEST PARK, BRISTOL, *March* 24, 1887.

THE NAME "OXFORD."

I ˆobserve that Mr. Henry Bradley says (*Academy*, March 12) : "For me, as for Mr. Mayhew, 'Oxford' means 'ford for oxen.'"

This is not the first time that I have found myself in the perilous position of differing from Mr. Bradley in a matter of this kind, nor the first time that I have also perilously differed from the Rev. Mr. Mayhew. I hope I am not guilty of a cumulative heresy in differing, as I now do, from both at once. I doubt, however, if in this case of Oxford "the obvious etymology is really the correct one."

I have several times exemplified that the most ancient names of many rivers were originally common to their trunks and their several branches, afterwards changed, in their several parts or members, often by mere dialectal or tribal variations of the original name, but sometimes having left traces of the earlier names in the names of places on their banks. Thus we have York on the part of the Eure now called Ouse ; Blanford = Vlanford = Alavna(ford),—perhaps at or near King Alfred's "Leonaford," where Asser visited him,—on the part of Ptolemy's Alauna that is now the Stour. Ile is a branch of the Ivel, the

K

Uxella of Ptolemy; and others might be observed. So, also, the river Ock, although it joins the Isis or Ouse at Abingdon, below Oxford, has left its name, Ocksford, there, as well as a transition form at Oseney. Like a tree, a river and its branches formed one object to its first namers, the explorers from its mouth.

In fact, Oxford is far older than is thought by the people who live there. The St. Ebb's dedication there is not the Lady of Coldingham and St. Abb's Head. South of Durham her name marks no spot of land in England; nor is there any name like it, or that is likely to be a variety of it, south of her monastery at Ebchester, in the bishopric of Durham, throughout all that largest area of England between that and Oxford, where—and at Shellswell, in the same county, —dedications of St. Ebb are found that have been erroneously Godsibbed to her, and the name accordingly reduced to her form. These are in the midst of an insulated cluster of impressions upon the land of the name of St. Abban, one of the Irish missionaries who have left their names so plentifully over the South and West of England. Both shores of the Severn estuary swarm with their names, and some are still discernible as having penetrated from that

inlet far into the land. The case of Maildulph=
Maeldubh, " Scotus," at Malmesbury, has overlapped
into our accepted secular history. Tewkesbury=
Theotisbyrg, is probably another from Toit of Inis
Toíte (Mart. of Donegal, September 7). However,
the two Oxfordshire St. Ebbs apparently form a part
of a group all within pastoral or missionary reach of
Abingdon, certainly known to have been originally
" Abbandun " ; and I believe the charters of
Abingdon, published in the " Rolls " series (not this
minute at hand), begin with a recital of the Celtic
tradition of St. Abban. A fourth of the cluster is a
place called St. Abbes, or " Tabs," near Ealing, four-
teen miles south of Abingdon. A fifth is " Abban
Crundel," near Bedwin (Cod. Dipl. No. 1,266). A
sixth, " Abban wylle," at Bensington (Cod. Dipl. No.
1,292). Mr. J. R. Green, indeed (" Making of England"),
seems to acknowledge the personality of the Celtic
colonist, but calls him " the *West-Saxon* Abba." But
Mr. Green was one of the now retreating " English
School," to whom all things were Saxon. At all
events, this cluster of his footsteps indicates a
missionary district—may we say an incipient *Paro-
echia*, or a " Christianitie," a name by which some
home, or central, archdeaconries are still known ?—

K 2

christianised by St. Abba. In this case Oxford must have existed, and been stamped with his name, in about the sixth century. St. Abb's Head exemplifies the reverse variation of the name of St. Ebb.

THOMAS KERSLAKE.

Bristol, *March* 12, 1887.

In support of the contention that Oxford means, say, Waterford or Watford, let me draw attention to the somewhat similar usage at Uxbridge. This small town stands on a river named the Colne, being one of several so named from a Roman colonia. Here the source was Verulamium, and the settlers squatted along the river banks as at Coln-brook, Colne London, Colney Street, &c. The river now reaches the Thames at Staines; but there is a small stream, once perhaps a main outlet of the Colne, which enters the Thames at Halliford, called the Exe, so I am informed. Here is a support and explanation of *Ux*bridge, similar to the occurrence of the Ock, at Abingdon; Ox, Ock, and Ux are connected like Exe, Usk, Isca, &c.

A. HALL.

London, *March* 18, 1887.

[*Academy, April* 2, 1887.]

I AM reminded of the old saying, and I feel tempted to exclaim, " Pereat Thomas Kerslakius, qui ante me mea dixit ! "

During the last week I have had pressing work; but I intended to send to the *Academy* to-day the following :—I have long thought " Oxford " to be " Ock's Ford." At Abingdon a stream called "Ock" (a stream-name in Devon also), which causes a street to be called Ock Street, falls into the river that flows down from Oxford; the latter stream, too, was, I have thought, called of old " Ock." With " Ock " I would compare Oxus, Ux-(bridge), Axe, Axus, Oaxes, Axius, Exe, Esk, Esque, Œscus, Usk, Isca or Isaca, Isac, Aach, Ash, &c.

In Prof. F. Max Müller's " Lectures on the Science of Language," sixth edition (1871), vol. ii., p. 580, is this :—

" The following local legend was sent me from Dorset :

" ' The Vale of Blackmore, in Dorset, was, till a late period, a vast forest, chiefly of oaks, the river Stour running through it. Hence, there were many oak-fords, fords by the oaks, which name is retained in several villages called Ockford. . . .' "

I think that the supposition that "Ockford" is " oak-ford " is a mistake, and that " Ock " in " Ock-ford " is another name for the river Stour.

I now add this : Mr. Kerslake says of " the river
Ock" that "it joins the Isis."   " Isis " is but an arti-
ficial name, manufactured in consequence of the mistaken notion that " Tamesis" is a compound of
" Thame" and " Isis."

J. HOSKYNS-ABRAHALL.

COMBE VICARAGE, near WOODSTOCK,
    March 19, 1887.

[*Academy, April* 2, 1887.]

IT seems to be a leading characteristic of the
Celtomaniac etymologisers that they never trouble to
ascertain the original form of the words about whose
origins they discourse, nor do they trouble their heads
about the value of vowels nor the presence of a few
inconvenient consonants.   Thus Mr. Kerslake does
not attempt to explain how " Ocksford " could ever
be written " Oxna-ford."   It is spelt " Oxene-ford "
in the Domesday Survey, which is surely the first book
a local etymologist should turn to.

Similarly, the Domesday orthography of Tewkesbury disposes of Mr. Kerslake's fanciful etymology
of that name.   It is therein written as " Teodeches-

berie" (fo. 163a, col. 2) and " Teodekesberie " (fo. 163b, col. 1). I do not suppose Mr. Kerslake will claim that " Teodek " contains the Irish " Toít. By the side of such a claim Malmesbury's derivation of the name from θεοτόκος (" Gesta Pontificum," §157, p. 295) is comparatively reasonable. Malmesbury writes the name " Theokesberia." " Teodekesberie " seems to be clearly enough the *burh* of a man named **þéod-ica*. The Anglo-Saxon names in *ica* or *uca*, later *cca*, appear in the eleventh and twelfth centuries with gen. in *-es*,[*] so that the gen. **þéodices* is easily accounted for.

It is rather vague to speak of " Oseney " as preserving the name " Ock" in " a transition form." Transition to what ? I do not know the earlier forms of " Oseney "; but, if they be anything like the present orthography, this name must surely contain the Anglo-Saxon personal name of *O'sa*, gen. *O'san*.

I do not think Mr. Kerslake is any happier with his etymology of Abingdon. *Abba* or *Æbba*, with its fem. *Abbe* or *Æbbe*, is a well-certificated Teutonic name occurring on the Continent as well as in

---

* See Birch, " Cart. Saxonicum," ii. 377, 17, " Tædduces stán," compared with the earlier " Tættucan stán " of ii. 94, 23. There are many more instances in the charters and in Domesday.

England. This being so, I see no reason to refer local names compounded with this personal name to an Irish saint, who was probably never in England in his life. It is true that the History of Abingdon derives the name of the place from *Abennus*, an Irish hermit who settled there in the time of Diocletian. Mr. Kerslake calls this "a Celtic tradition." How would he describe the mythical British history of Geoffrey of Monmouth? For one of Geoffrey's creations, the all-powerful British king Lucius, is referred to in almost the same breath as Abbenus. Hence it is clear that this Abingdon tale cannot have been concocted until after the publication of Geoffrey's marvellous history. The further conclusion that Abenus is as mythical as Lucius himself seems to me unavoidable. I do not believe that Abenus is a whit more historic than the hermit Theokus whom the monks of Tewkesbury invented to account for the name of their monastery (" Monasticon," ii. 59). The inventors of this venerable Tewkesbury hermit were ignorant of the fact that the name was originally *þeodices-burh*, and I hold that their Abingdon brethren of the twelfth or thirteenth century were similarly ignorant that *Æbba*, m., and *Æbbe*, fem., were Anglo-Saxon personal names.

Mr. Green may have been too enthusiastic in his love for the West-Saxons to avoid occasional errors ; but I do not think that Mr. Kerslake has convicted him of an error in the present case, for " Abba " is certainly as much a West-Saxon name as " William " is a modern English one. If the " English School " be " now retreating " (which I very much doubt), I do not think they need fear any great loss in their retreat from such hasty etymological guesses as Mr. Kerslake here presents to us.

W. H. STEVENSON.

Nottingham, *March* 21, 1887.

[*Academy*, *April* 2, 1887.]

Why are we told that the name " Oxeneford," as found in Domesday, must have been the " original form " ?

I quite admit that the use of *ox* or *oxen*, in this connection, is justified, but it is not of necessity primitive. Prof. Skeat quotes " *oxa*, plural *oxan*," as the true form, where *oxene* is Middle English ; and, certainly, the castle-mound at Oxford is early Saxon, if not British.

I have the following Celtic forms :—

1. " Caer *Pen*halgoed " ; this I would connect with *Head*ington and the upper part of Oxford, where the ground forms a peninsula, a spit or headland between the Cherwell and the Isis.

2. " Rhydychain," a counterpart to the Domesday form, meaning " Oxford."

3. " Caer Wysog," a term ˌof watery omen ; which seems to apply to the confluence of waters about Oseney, Binsey, Hinksey, all of which I take to have been at one time isolated sandbanks, protruding amid the wide waste of waters.

I propose to account for the transition meaning of Oxene by the Roman portway which ran southwards in this direction from Heyford; at Kirtlington it joined the Akeman Street from Bicester to Cirencester. It is contended that this thoroughfare crossed the Port-meadow at a fordway, which points directly to Cumnor, Wantage, and the Berkshire Ridgeway ; but I do not connect the names. Portways are found all over Britain; and I connect them with the Latin *portare*, as meaning a line for traffic, in contra-distinction to the imperial highways, maintained for troops and couriers. The portmeadow is local, so to speak, a *town* meadow, or fair-mead, as found elsewhere.

My point is that these Portways, Ridgeways, &c., were freely used by drovers ; but all this sounds late, for the ancient Britons, who navigated the rivers in their coracles, had no cattle fairs to draw Highland drovers southwards with their beasties. But these ancient Britons named their rivers. So with regard to Oseney, why not Ousen-ey, *i.e.*, " ey," an island, *ouse*, a river-name : we have

Ousby, *cf.* Oseby
Ousden
Ouseburn, *cf.* Osbourn-by } = Ouse, Usk, Ock,
Ousefleet, *cf.* O-Springe   Isis, Ixa, &c.
Ouseley

Under improved navigation the Thames or Isis is now known as the *old* river at Oxford, and a dirty hole it is in parts.

A. HALL.

London, *April* 2, 1887.

[*" Academy," April* 9, 1887.]

I LOOK upon the name as transmitted traditionally through the mouths of those who have been using it for their daily purposes of life through from ten to fifteen centuries to be a better text of it than that of

Domesday, or the other written examples which Mr. Stevenson calls "the original form" of it. It comes from an issue much nearer the source. This career has no doubt qualified it; but it has escaped pedantic meanings that may have been infused into it by the ingenuity of clerkship, analagous to canting heraldry. The names of rivers have had much more to do with such matters than the most trivial and ordinary uses of bucolic life. If I had been a Celtomaniac, I would have rested upon the Welsh form, "Rhydychain," which I believe would have thrown me directly into your correspondent's embraces.

As to Tewkesbury, Mr. Stevenson may see what perhaps he would call an "original form," which it is not—but, perhaps, better than Domesday, and still better than William of Malmesbury,—among the Additions, p. 584, second edition of Weever's "Funeral Monument"—"Theotisbyrg." For which I refer again to what I wrote before, as I do also to what I said about Abban. Attentive reading is better than reprinting.

Mr. Hoskins-Abrahall, by his Latin imprecation, confesses alliance with me, but he says "Isis" is but an artifical name. Is he sure of this? It is more likely to be a variety of the frequent "Ouse," which has left a jetsam in "Osency." There is an Ouse in Sussex, having on its banks "*Is*field," "Lew*es*," and " South*ease*," within its short course : not to speak of " *Uck*field," which may pair off with our " Ock."

THOMAS KERSLAKE.

BRISTOL, *April* 4, 1887.

[" *Academy*, *April* 9, 1887.]

" *THAMES*" *AND* " *THAME*."

THE oldest forms of these names occur respectively as " Tamesis" and " Tam " or " Tame " (as in " æt Tame " of the Anglo-Saxon Chronicle, A.D. 791). The present mode of spelling may, perhaps, be due to the following cause. Prof. Earle (if I am not mistaken) has referred " Tackley" (Oxon.) to " æt-âc-lea," where the prep. " æt" is untranslated ; hence the collateral forms of " Tackley" and "Oakley." Now, just as " Tackley," or " Taclea," was known at an early period to be derived from " 'tac-lea" (æt-âc-lea), why should not " Tame " at the same time have been considered as a derivation from " 't-âme" for " æt-âme," which in its turn was regarded as a corruption of " æt-hâme"

(= at the "homestead," &c.) ?   If this assumption be correct, then the change from " Tame " to " Thame " is accounted for.   The river which was thought to owe its name to the town then became the " Thame " (originally " Tam "), and " Tamise " (Temese) became " Thames " (Themese) by assimilation to " Thame."

E. SIBREE.

Oxford, *March* 31, 1887.

[" *Academy*," *April* 9, 1887.]

THE NAMES "OXFORD" AND "TEWKESBURY."

It is a work of supererogation to protest against Mr. Kerslake's excuse for taking " Oxford " to be the original form of the name.   His plea that this is the form " transmitted traditionally through the mouths of those who have been using it for their daily purposes of life through from ten to fifteen centuries " is inadmissible, for it is based upon an assumption that is opposed to all documentary evidence.   The original form of the name was undoubtedly " Oxnaford," and it is idle to speak of " pedantic meanings that may have been infused into it by the ingenuity of clerkship, analogous to canting heraldry."   The Domesday form is valuable as being a foreigner's representation of the sound of the name, and it is perfectly in accord with the phonology of the Domesday scribes. I may explain, for the benefit of Mr. Hall, that *oxna* is the gen. pl. of *oxa*. Not only is the form "Oxna-ford" well authenticated, but the change from that form to "Oxford" is perfectly regular. I might quote a score of instances from the Anglo-Saxon charters where an *n* has dropped off from the end of the first member of a compound, but the instance of "Folke-stone" from Anglo-Saxon "Folcan-stán" will suffice for my present purpose. This loss of the *n* had already taken place in Northumbrian in Bede's time, and it gradually spread to the other dialects. It was a result of the wearing down of the weak declension and its gradual absorption into the strong. I assume in the present instance that the weak gen. pl. has undergone the same process as the gen. sing., or that the two have been identified. Neither of these is a very violent assumption. It is clear, therefore, that "Oxford" is both the historical and the phonological representative of the Anglo-Saxon "Oxna-ford." That name can only mean "the ford of oxen." Mr. Kerslake objects that "the names of rivers have had much more to do with such matters (as local names) than the most trivial and ordinary uses of bucolic life." This is a very elastic assertion, which would be very difficult to prove or to disprove. To benefit Mr. Kerslake's case at all, it is necessary to absolutely preclude any local name derived from the "ordinary uses of bucolic life." The fact that many local names are derived from such sources at once disposes of his plea. As an unimaginative follower of the "English School," it seems to me that the obvious etymology of the following local names is the real one, and that they are analagous to "Oxford": Horspath, Horsforth, Oxlode, Sheepwash. There is an "Oxenfoord" Castle in Edinburghshire, but there appears to be no village of this name. Perhaps Mr. Kerslake or Mr. Hall can fix Welsh etymologies to these names, for one of the main attractions of the pseudo-Celtic school of etymology seems to lie in its ability to find Celtic etymologies for any word, however Teutonic it may look.*

* When we are gravely told that "Eastbourne" is Celtic, as we are in Palmer's "Dictionary of Folk Etymology," it becomes a question whether we are to abandon this Celtic mania, or give up the philological conquests of the last fifty years. I see, from a communication of Mr. Mayhew's in last week's *Notes and Queries*, that this dictionary is the source of the idea that "Oxford" is derived from the Ock, and that the same delusive list of parallel names is there adduced as has figured in this discussion.

Against the cumulative evidence of history, of phonology, and of analogy, Mr. Kerslake propounds an etymology that is sapped by fatal objections like the following : (1) there is no evidence whatever of the name ever having been " Ocks-ford " ; (2) there is no necessity for the *s*, for, according to analogy and common sense, the name should be " Ock-ford " ; (3) there is not the faintest evidence that the Isis was ever known as the Ock. Really, the etymological ideas of Mr. Kerslake and Mr. Hall seem to be as loose and accommodating as those of Verstegan.

With regard to the name " Tewkesbury," Mr. Kerslake, if he be true to his own principles, has no right to etymologise from any other than the modern form of the name ; for if " Oxford " is to be preferred to " Oxna-ford," on the ground that it is the form " traditionally transmitted through the mouths of those who have been using it for their daily purposes of life through from ten to fifteen centuries," so must " Tewkesbury " override any forms like " Theotis-byrg." A principle that can be enforced or ignored at the whim of its formulator cannot exact much respect.

Mr. Kerslake refers me to Weever for the form

" Theotisbyrg," which he considers disposes of the Domesday form of the name. I maintain that the Domesday form is the more valuable; indeed, it is of the highest value, as being the attempt of a foreigner to represent the sound of the name. The inscription in Weever is very little older than the date of Domesday, and it may be even younger. The inscription as printed by Weever has been confessedly tampered with. Altogether, it is a suspicious piece of evidence which cannot be allowed to outweigh the unimpeachable testimony of Domesday.

Since writing my first letter, I have discovered important evidence in support of the etymology of Tewkesbury therein propounded. Indeed, it would be more accurate to say that this evidence forestalls my etymology. In Liebermann's " Ungedruckte Anglo-Normannische Geschichtsquellen," p. 15, is printed a chronicle from Cott. MS. Vitellius. C. viii., a MS. assigned by Sir T. Duffus Hardy to the early part of the twelfth century. This chronicle, which Lieber-mann calls " Annales de ecclesiis et regnis Anglorum," was compiled in the diocese of Worcester. It contains frequent quotations from Malmesbury's " Gesta Pontificum," including § 157, which contains Malmesbury's derivation of Tewkesbury from θεοτόκος.* This quotation is followed by these words : " Monasterium etiam quod ' *Theodekesberia* ' vocatur ipsa continet provincia, quod *Theodokus* quidam quondam construxit, *a quo et nomen accepit*," &c. (p. 23). Now this *Theodokus* is merely a latinisation of *þéod-oc, a regular late form of *þéod-ica ; that is, the *k* diminutive has lost its final *a*, and has gone over to the strong declension. All this is perfectly regular, even to the substitution of *o* for *u* or *i* as the connecting vowel between the stem and the suffix. Every stage in this process can be clearly traced among the names compounded with this *k* diminutive. The following instances are so much to the point that I think no more need be said : A.D. 1045, *Dodica* episcopus, "Codex Diplomaticus," iv. 99, 5 ; A.D. 1038, *Duduc* episcopus, *id.*, iv. 60, 15 ; A.D. 1043, *Dudoca* episcopus, *id.*, iv. 75, 17. All these forms refer to one man. Therefore I maintain that the chronicler's *Theodokus* is a real name and not an eponym. It may be objected that the chronicler's etymology is weakened by his similar derivation of " Akemannes-

---

* It is clear that Malmesbury must have had such a form as *Theodekes-beria*, and not his own "Theokesberia," in his mind when he propounded this etymology.

cestre " from a founder named " Akemannus,"* " ut ab antiquis accepimus " (p. 19), and of Wight, "a rege Britonum, qui Wicht nominabatur." But I do not attach much weight to this objection, for even the most unscientific etymologist may occasionally hit upon a correct etymology, and in this case the derivation is from a *bonâ-fide* personal name. It might have had, in addition, the support of local tradition. According to my experience, far more English local names are derived from personal names than from any other source. Prof. Skeat informs me that his studies in local etymology have led him to the same conclusion.

In support of his etymology of Abingdon from the Irish *Abban*, Mr. Kerslake adduces the instance of Malmesbury from *Maeldubh*. He does not see that this is in itself an argument against him ; for, although *Maeldubh* is a Celtic name, it is here compounded with the English gen. *-es;* so that if Abingdon had been derived from *Abban*, the name would have been,

---

* Is it certain that this etymology is wrong ? No satisfactory origin for this name has yet been propounded. Bede's *Tunna-caestir* ("H. E.," iv. 22) proves that *ceaster* was sometimes linked with a personal name. There are several Anglo-Saxon names in *ác*, so that a name *A'c-mann* is not altogether impossible or improbable.

according to rule, *Abban-es-dún*, instead of *Abban-dún*. There is, however, no trace whatever of any such form; and Mr. Kerslake's etymology may be safely consigned to the limbo that has received so many similar "Celtic" etymologies of Teutonic words.

W. H. STEVENSON.

Nottingham, *April* 14, 1887.

[*Academy, April* 30, 1887.]

CONCLUSION.

I WOULD here offer a few friendly words to the political separatists. Great Britain and Ireland belong to the great European family of States, all of which, except this country, are fully armed for any contingency. Great Britain has a smaller population than those military States, and cannot therefore afford to tolerate separatist notions in any part of the Empire. The desire for a partition reminds one of the old story of the two mothers, and King Solomon's judgment against the one who was willing to see the baby cut asunder.

The British Isles contain the descendants of many races, amalgamated into one nationality, called in England " English," in Scotland "Scottish," in Ireland " Irish."

All have one Queen, one country, and, *united*, one national interest.

To the Irish separatists I would point out that if they succeeded in their mistaken enterprise, the numerous lucrative posts held by Irishmen in England, in India, and in the British Colonies, would no longer fall to their share.

BERNARD QUARITCH.

May, 1887.

TABLE OF CONTENTS.

PAGE

RACES OF THE BRITISH ISLES:

LUBBOCK (Sir John)—Letter to the *Times*, March 18, 1887   7

———————————————— March 25 ,,   15

———————————————— March 31 ,,   34

———————————————— April   9 ,,   38

BRYCE (J.), M.P.—Letter to the *Times*, March 21 ,,   13

———————————————— March 28 ,,   22

———————————————— April   2 ,,   36

M.P.—Letter to the *Times* ... ... March 25 ,,   21

BEDDOE (Dr. John)—Letter to the *Times*, March   ,,   28

———————————————— April   9 ,,   40

THE DUKE OF ARGYLL—Letter to the
     Times ... ... March 31 ,,   29

MAXWELL (Herbert E.)—Letter to Sir
     John Lubbock ... ... March 31 ,,   41

HUXLEY (Professor)—Letter to Sir John
     Lubbock ... ... May   2 ,,   42

PLACE AND RIVER NAMES IN ENGLAND:

KERSLAKE (Thomas)—Gyfla, the Scír of the Ivel Valley   47

————————————Letter to Mr. Quaritch, March
       24, 1887   62

————————————The Name "Oxford," *Academy*,
       April 2, April 9, 1887   65, 75

HALL (A.)—Letters to the *Academy*, April 2, April 9,
     1887 ... ... 68, 73

ABRAHALL (J. Hoskyns)—Letter to the *Academy*, April
     2, 1887   69

QUARITCH (Bernard)—Letter to Mr. Kerslake, March
     23, 1887   61

SIBREE (E.)—Letter to the *Academy*, April 9, 1887   ...   77

STEVENSON (W. H.)—Letter to the *Academy*, April 2, 1887   70

———————————————— April 30 ,,   78

QUARITCH'S REPRINTS.

I.—VESPUCCI (AMERIGO) LETTERA delle Isole nova-
mente trovate, sm. 4to. Florence, 1505, *facsimile
reprint*, price £5. 5s.

———— the same, translated, with notes, sm. 4to.,
£2. 12s. 6d.

II.—LACE BOOK : Studio delle Virtuose Dame, dissegn.
da Parasole, Roma, 1597, oblong 4to., *facsimile
reprint*, 21s.

III.—LACE BOOK : La Gloria et l'Honore de Ponti
tagliati, M. Pagan, Venetia, 1558, sm. 4to., *facsimile
reprint*, 21s.

IV.—FALCONRY: Perfect Booke for kepinge of SPAR-
HAWKES or GOSHAWKES, written about 1575, now
printed from the original MS., with Introduction
and Glossary by J. E. Harting, 1 vol. 4to., 1886,
hf. bd., £1. 1s.

WYMAN AND SONS, PRINTERS, GREAT QUEEN STEET, LONDON, W.C.

www.ingramcontent.com/pod-product-compliance
Lightning Source LLC
Chambersburg PA
CBHW032348020726
47499CB00008B/2668